BONANZA GOLD

PIERRE BERTON

BONANZA GOLD

ILLUSTRATIONS BY HENRY VAN DER LINDE

An M&S Paperback Original from
McClelland & Stewart Inc.
The Canadian Publishers

An M&S Paperback Original from McClelland & Stewart Inc.

First printing November 1991

Canadian Cataloguing in Publication Data

Berton, Pierre, 1920–
  Bonanza gold

(Adventures in Canadian history. The great
Klondike gold rush)
"An M&S paperback original".
Includes index.
ISBN 0-7710-1432-5

1. Henderson, Robert, d. 1933 – Juvenile literature.
2. Carmack, George W. (George Washington), 1860–
1922 – Juvenile literature. 3. Klondike River
Valley (Yukon) – Gold discoveries – Juvenile
literature. 4. Gold miners – Yukon Territory –
Biography – Juvenile literature. I. Van der Linde,
Henry. II. Title. III. Series: Berton, Pierre,
1920– . Adventures in Canadian history. The
great Klondike gold rush.

FC4022.3.B47 1991   j971.9'102   C91-094456-3
F1095.K5B47 1991

Series design by Tania Craan
Text design by Martin Gould
Cover illustration by David Bathurst
Interior illustrations by Henry Van Der Linde
Maps by James Loates
Editor: Peter Carver

Typesetting by Pickwick
Printed and bound in Canada

McClelland & Stewart Inc.
The Canadian Publishers
481 University Avenue
Toronto, Ontario
M5G 2E9

CONTENTS

Maps appear on pages 14 and 66

Overview
The golden highway

A LINE OF GOLD STRETCHES north along the continental spine from the land of the Incas in Peru to the chill sands of Norton Sound on the Bering Sea, opposite Siberia.

People have searched for gold ever since the fabled days of *El Dorado*, the legendary treasure city of South America. There was gold there in the mountains – the Incas made jewellery from it that can be seen to this day – and there was gold farther north in Mexico, the land of the Aztecs.

Gold in the Sierras produced the great California stampede in 1849. Gold strikes in Arizona and Colorado helped make the American West wild. There was gold in the Fraser River of British Columbia and gold in the fabled Cariboo, gold at Lake Atlin on the Yukon border, gold in the sandbars of the Yukon River, gold along the watershed of the Klondike and the Fortymile, gold in Alaska at Fairbanks, on the Tanana, at Circle City, and at Nome near the mouth of the Yukon.

The gold had bubbled up, hot and molten within the

backbone of the continent. Over the eons, as the mountains were ground down by wind, water, and ice, the gold was ground down too, and washed down the mountainsides in ancient streams. The coarse gold, being heaviest, was caught in the crevices of the bedrock. The finer gold was pushed farther down the slopes, while the finest gold – fine as sifted flour – ended in the sandbars at the mouths of creeks and rivers. There it stayed as the streams changed course, while the vegetation turned to soil and covered the old creek beds in a mantle of clay. To find it, men had to burrow deep into the bowels of the earth, building shafts to bedrock and then scraping out tunnels or "drifts" to find the old channels where the "pay-streak" glittered.

Men still stampede for gold today whenever a new find is announced, but it isn't the same. In the nineteenth century, before the airplane and the helicopter, every gold strike was remote. But none was quite so remote as the Klondike, on a river that wasn't even named on the maps.

There are several reasons why the Klondike gold rush appeals to us as romantic. For one, it contained the richest ground in history. Second, it was far enough away to be glamorous, yet still within the reach of those men and women determined enough to get there by foot and home-made boat.

Finally, it was a "poor man's" stampede. One or two men could actually sink a shaft in the frozen ground, find the pay-streak at bedrock, and haul up the gold by themselves.

The only capital they needed was money for food and enough left over to build a cabin and a sluicebox. Thus paupers became millionaires, almost overnight – and that was the appeal of the gold find on the Klondike in 1896.

CHAPTER ONE
A fateful meeting

THIS IS A STORY OF A MAN who spent all his life searching for gold, only to let a fortune slip through his fingers because he made a racist remark about Indians. Robert Henderson didn't like Indians. That cost him dearly. If he hadn't opened his mouth he would have become a millionaire.

He hailed from Big Island off the coast of Nova Scotia. A lighthouse-keeper's son, he could scarcely remember the time when he hadn't thought of gold. As a child he'd read Alaskan histories and wandered about Nova Scotia searching for gold, finding nothing. As a boy of 14, he decided to spend all his life seeking gold.

He thought that the southern hemisphere held out the best hope, and so signed aboard a sailing ship to search the seven seas. He panned and picked in New Zealand and Australia and other corners of the globe and found nothing. After five years, he tried the northern hemisphere, working his way up through the Rocky Mountain states to the mines of Colorado. Then, after fourteen years of fruitless search, he was carried north with a human tide flowing towards Alaska. He searched for gold on the Pelly River, a great tributary of the mighty Yukon, but found no gold in the Pelly. And still he kept looking.

He was tall and lean, with a gaunt, hawk's face, fierce brows and piercing eyes. His full moustache, drooping slightly at the edges, gave him a stern look that revealed his Scottish ancestry. He wore his broad-brimmed miner's hat proudly, as if it were a kind of badge. All his life he wore it, on city streets and wilderness pathways. It proclaimed to the world that Robbie Henderson was a prospector.

In 1894, he reached the trading post of Joseph Ladue on the upper Yukon River. Ladue was at the mouth of the Sixtymile River sixty miles (100 km) upstream from Fort Reliance, and Henderson persuaded Ladue to back him in his search. Ladue had spent twelve years on the river. He too had been obsessed with the idea of gold. He was a stocky man of French (not Quebec) ancestry, and gold had a very real meaning for him. Without it he could not marry his sweetheart, Anna Mason, whose wealthy parents continued to think of him as a penniless drifter. She was faithfully waiting for him, three thousand miles (4,800 km) away, while he sought his fortune in a plain log cabin on the banks of the Yukon.

That post lay about a hundred miles (160 km) from the border between Yukon and Alaska. Between that point and the border, two other rivers flowed into the Yukon – the

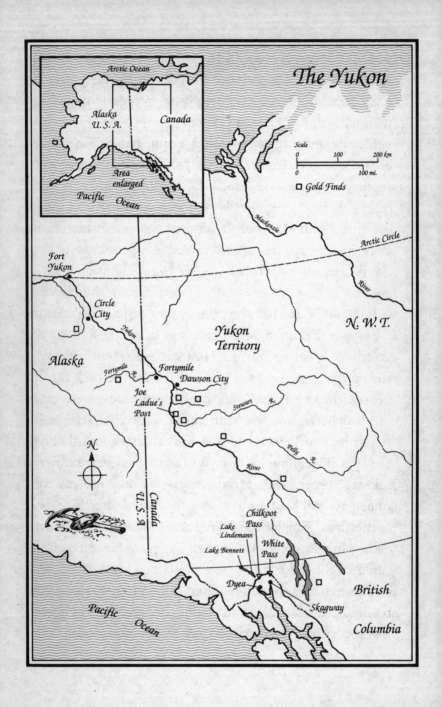

Indian River about thirty miles (50 km) downstream, and the Thron-diuck River, another thirty miles farther down. Ladue had explored the Thron-diuck in the old days, and had sworn that there was gold in its streams. Now, however, he believed that the neighbouring Indian River was ankle-deep in nuggets. He told every prospector who stopped at his post, including Henderson, that it was rich with gold.

"Let me prospect for you," Henderson told Jack Ladue. "If it's good for me, it's good for you. I'm a determined man, I won't starve."

And so, for the next two years, Robert Henderson stubbornly combed the Indian River and its tributaries looking for gold. He searched with that same restlessness that had governed his life, shifting from creekbed to creekbed but never settling for long at any given spot.

He found gold, but he never found enough to satisfy him. On the sand bars of the main river he found gold as delicate as lace. He dragged his sled up Quartz Creek, and here he found gold as coarse as sand. It still was not what he was seeking. Possibly, even if he had found a cache of twenty-dollar gold pieces or a mountain of solid gold, he would have felt vaguely disappointed, because with Henderson it was the search itself that counted.

Bad luck dogged him, but he didn't give up. He suffered the agonies of leg cramps from wading in the chilling streams, and snow-blindness from the glare on the white slopes. On Australia Creek he had the terrifying experience of falling across a broken branch, being impaled through the calf and hanging over the rushing torrent like a slab of beef on a butcher's hook. For fourteen days he lay crippled in his bivouac. Then he was away again, living off the land, eating caribou or ptarmigan, limping through the forests or travelling the shallow streams in a crude boat made from the skins of animals.

Occasionally he would raise his eyes northward to examine a curious round mountain – known as a "dome" – whose summit rose above the other hills. The creeks of Indian River flowed down the flanks of this dome, and Henderson guessed that on the other side more nameless creeks flowed into another river – probably the Throndiuck, or "Klondike," as the miners mispronounced it. At last his prospector's curiosity got the better of him. He climbed the dome to see what was on the other side.

When he reached the summit a sight of breath-taking majesty met his gaze. To the north a long line of glistening snow-capped peaks marched off like soldiers to vanish beyond the lip of the horizon. In every other direction the violet hills rolled on as far as the eye could see, hill upon hill, valley upon valley, gulch upon gulch – and each hill about the same height as its neighbour. The whole effect, seen through half-closed eyes, was of a great plateau creased and gouged and furrowed by centuries of running water.

From the summit on which Henderson was standing that spring of 1895, the creeks radiated out like the spokes of a wheel, with himself at the hub, three falling off towards the Indian River and three more, on the far side, running to some unknown stream. He could not know it, but these were six of the richest gold-bearing creeks in the world. They wound through beds of black muck and thick moss, bordered by rank grasses from which the occasional moose lifted its dripping snout. They twisted across flat valley floors whose sides, notched by steep gulches, rose in steps marking the pathway of once mighty tributaries.

Almost at Henderson's feet a deep cleft dropped off from the dome. He walked down a little way and dipped his pan into a small creek. When the gravel and sand washed away, there was about eight cents' worth of gold left behind. Henderson weighed it out with the pair of scales that every prospector carried. *Eight cents to the pan!* In those days, that was a good prospect; he felt that he had at last found what he was looking for.

Back he went over the mountain to the Indian River, where about twenty men, lured by Ladue's tales, were toiling away on the sand-bars. He persuaded three to return with him to the creek, which he named "Gold Bottom" because, as he said wistfully, "I had a daydream that when I got my shaft down to bedrock it might be like the streets of New Jerusalem."

By midsummer of 1896 the four men had taken out $750, and it was time for Henderson to head back to Ladue's post for more supplies. To each man he met he told the story of a V-shaped valley back in the hills. This free

Robert Henderson pans for gold on Gold Bottom. But the real treasure was on Hunker and Bonanza Creeks.

exchange of information was part of the prospector's code, in which Henderson fiercely believed. He not only told strangers of the gold, but he also urged them to turn back in their tracks and stake claims by hammering in peeled log posts at the four corners of their five-hundred-foot (150 m) find. In this way he emptied the settlement at the mouth of the Sixtymile. Every man except Ladue headed downstream.

His order filled, Henderson drifted back the way he had come in his skin boat. It was late summer, and the water was low. The Indian River was so shallow that Henderson, fearing he might tear his craft to shreds trying to navigate it, determined to continue on down the Yukon towards the Thron-diuck, guessing correctly that Gold Bottom Creek must flow into it. Thus, on a fateful summer's day he approached his meeting with George Washington Carmack. The bitter memory of that moment was to haunt Henderson all the days of his life.

As he brought his boat around a broad curve in the river and past a rocky bluff, he could hear on his right the roar of the Thron-diuck, or Klondike, as it poured out from between the flat-topped hills to join the Yukon. Directly before him now, just beyond the Klondike's mouth, rose a tapering mountain, its pointed peak naked of timber. Slashed across its flank was an immense and evil scar in the shape of a stretched moose hide, the product of slow erosion by underground springs. At its base, a wedge of flat swampland covered with scrub timber bordered the riverbank for a mile and a half (2.4 km) – ugly, foul, and mosquito-infested. It seemed an almost impossible place for settlement, yet this was to be the site of the gaudiest city in the North.

The Thron-diuck was known as the finest salmon stream in the Yukon – hence its name: an Indian word meaning "Hammer-Water" which, pronounced in the native fashion, sounded like a man in the throes of strangulation. It was so called because the Indians had hammered stakes across the shallow mouth in order to spread their nets. Henderson could smell the stench of the fish drying in the sun, and on the bank just below the river's mouth he could see a white man moving about.

The idea of anyone fishing for a living when there was gold to be had appalled him. He later recalled his first thought: "There's a poor devil who hasn't struck it."

As was his habit, he decided to share his good fortune with the fisherman, and a moment later he was up on the bank talking to George Washington Carmack, or "McCormick," as he was often called.

The two men, who would later be called "co-discoverers of the Klondike" and around whom so much controversy was to swirl, were opposites in almost every way. Henderson, with his chiselled features, serious and intense, bore little resemblance to the easy-going, ever optimistic salmon fisherman with his heavy jowls, his sleepy eyes, and his rather plump features. But they had one quality in common: an incurable restlessness controlled their lives.

Carmack was the child of an earlier gold rush. His father had crossed the western plains in a covered wagon in '49, heading for California, and Carmack had been born at Port Costa, across the bay from San Francisco. He had gone to work at 16 years of age aboard the ferryboats, shipped to Alaska as a dishwasher on a man-of-war, jumped ship at Juneau, and pushed steadily north. In 1887 William Ogilvie, the Canadian surveyor, encountered him at Dyea. By that time Carmack could speak both the Chilkoot and the Tagish dialects, and had considerable influence over the Han or "Stick" Indians from the interior or the "Stick" country.

At a time and place when every man was a prospector, Carmack appeared to be a misfit. He alone of all men did not want gold. Instead he wanted to be an Indian in a land where the natives were generally scorned by the white man and the white word "Siwash" was racist. His wife, Kate, a member of the Tagish tribe, was the daughter of a chief, and it was Carmack's ambition to be chief himself. (Among the Tagishes, descent is through the chief's sister.)

He worked with the other Indians as a packer on the Chilkoot Pass, and by the time he moved into the interior with his wife and her two brothers he had three or four children of mixed blood. He had grown an Indian-type moustache that drooped over his lips Oriental style, and when anybody said to him: "George, you're getting more like an Indian every day," he took it as a compliment. He did not in the least mind his nicknames, "Stick George" and "Siwash George," for he considered himself a true Indian and he was proud of it.

While other men scrabbled and mucked in the smoky shafts of Alaskan mining camps, Siwash George was slipping up and down the river with Indian comrades. His easy-going mood matched that of the natives, who were a different breed from the fiercely competitive and ambitious Tlingit tribes of the coast.

When it suited Carmack, he bragged of gold discoveries he had made. It was certainly true that he had discovered a seam of coal on the Yukon River, but nobody took him seriously as a prospector, including Carmack himself. In the words of a Mounted Police sergeant at Fortymile, the nearest mining camp to the Alaska-Yukon border, he was a man "who would never allow himself to be beaten and always tried to present his fortunes in the best possible light." The men at Fortymile summed him up more tersely with a new nickname. They called him "Lying George."

Yet he was no dummy. He had an organ, of all things, in his cabin near Five Finger Rapids on the Yukon, and a library that included such journals as *Scientific American* and *Review of Reviews*. He like to converse on scientific topics and, occasionally, as on Christmas Eve in 1888, he wrote sad, sentimental poetry. ("A whisper comes from the tall old spruce, And my soul from pain is free: For I know when they kneel together to-night, They'll all be praying for me.")

He was also something of a mystic. In May of 1896 he was sitting on the bank of the Yukon near the ruins of old Fort

Selkirk at the mouth of the Pelly, and here, if one believes his later recollections, he had strange feelings. He stared into the blazing sunset and came to the conclusion that something unusual was about to take place in his life. On a whim he took his only coin, a silver dollar, from his pocket and threw it in the air. If it came down heads, he told himself, he would go back up the river; but if it showed tails, he would go downstream to test whatever fate had in store for him. Tails it was, and Carmack loaded his boat and started to drift the two-hundred-odd miles (320 km) to Fortymile.

That night he had a vivid dream in which he saw himself seated on the banks of a stream watching grayling shoot the rapids. Suddenly the fish scattered in fright and two enormous king salmon shot upstream and came to a dead stop in front of him. In place of scales they were armoured in gold nuggets and their eyes were twenty-dollar gold pieces. It reveals a great deal about Carmack that he took this as a sign that he go fishing; prospecting never entered his head. He determined to catch salmon on the Thron-diuck and sell it for dog-feed. So here he was, with his catch hanging to dry under a small birch lean-to, when Robert Henderson encountered him.

His Indian friends had joined him at the Klondike's mouth: Skookum Jim, a giant of a man, supremely handsome with his high cheek-bones, his eagle's nose, and his fiery black eyes – straight as a gun-barrel, powerfully built, and known as the best hunter and trapper on the river; Tagish Charley, lean and lithe as a panther, and, in Carmack's phrase, "alert as a weasel"; the silent, plump Kate with her straight black hair; and Carmack's daughter, known as Graphie Gracey because no white man could pronounce her real name. It was this group that Henderson approached with news of the strike at Gold Bottom. Carmack later set down his version of the conversation, which does not differ substantially from Henderson's briefer account:

"Hello, Bob! Where in the world did you drop from, and where do you think you're going?"

"Just came down from Ogilvie; I'm going up the Klondike."

"What's the idea, Bob?"

"There's been a prospect found in a small creek that heads up against the Dome. I think it empties into the Klondike about fifteen miles up, and I'm looking for a better way to get there than going over the mountains from the Indian River."

"Got any kind of a prospect?"

"We don't know yet. We can get a prospect on the surface. When I left, the boys were running up an open cut to get to bedrock."

"What are the chances to locate up there? Everything staked?"

Henderson glanced over at the two Indians who were standing nearby. Then he uttered the phrase that probably cost him a fortune. "There's a chance for you, George, but I don't want any damn Siwashes staking on that creek."

*Robert Henderson, meeting with Carmack and Skookum Jim,
suggests they try their luck on Rabbit Creek.*

He pushed his boat into the water and headed up the Klondike. But his final remark rankled.

"What's matter dat white man?" Skookum Jim asked, speaking in Chinook, the pidgin tongue of the traders that prevailed on the river. "Him killet Inchen moose, Inchen caribou, ketchet gold Inchen country, no liket Inchen staket claim, wha for, no good."

"Never mind, Jim," said Carmack lightly. "This is a big country. We'll go and find a creek of our own."

And, as it turned out, it was to be as simple as that.

CHAPTER TWO

Striking it rich

CARMACK DID NOT immediately follow Henderson's suggestion to go upriver and stake at Gold Bottom. He was less interested in gold than he was in logs, which he hoped to chop on Rabbit Creek, a tributary of the Klondike, and float down to the mill at Fortymile near the border for $25 per thousand feet (305 m).

Skookum Jim had already explored the creek and in passing had panned out some colours, for, just as Carmack wished to be an Indian, Jim longed to be a white man – in other words, a prospector. He differed from the others in his tribe in that he displayed the white man's kind of ambition. He had, in fact, earned his nickname of Skookum (meaning "husky") by his feat of packing the record load of 156 pounds (71 kg) of bacon across the steep Chilkoot Pass that led across the mountains into the heart of the Canadian Yukon. In vain he tried to interest Carmack in the prospects along Rabbit Creek; Carmack was not intrigued.

It was as much Carmack's restless nature as his desire for fortune that took him and the Indians to the site of

Henderson's strike some days after the meeting at the Klondike's mouth. They did not follow the river but decided to strike up the valley of Rabbit Creek, which led to the high ridge separating the Klondike and the Indian watersheds. The ridge led to the head of Gold Bottom.

They poled up the Klondike for two miles (3 km), left their boat, shouldered their packs, and began to trudge through the wet mosses and black muck and the great clumps of grass that marked the mouth of the Rabbit. As they went they prospected, dipping their pans into the clear water that rippled in the sunlight over sands white with quartz. As Carmack sat on his haunches, twirling the gold-pan, he began to recite Hamlet's soliloquy, "To be or not to be," for he felt that all prospecting was a gamble.

"Wa for you talket dat cultus wa wa?" Tagish Charley asked him. "I no see um gold."

"That's all right, Charley," Carmack told him. "I makum Boston man's medicine."

He raised the pan with its residue of black sand.

"Spit in it, boys, for good luck."

They spat, and then Carmack panned out the sand and raised the pan to show a tiny stream of colour.

On they trudged, stopping occasionally to pan again, finding minute pieces of gold, wondering whether or not to stake. They came to a fork in the frothing creek where another branch bubbled in from the south, and here they paused momentarily. They did not know it, but at that instant, they were standing on the richest ground in the world. There was gold all about them, not only beneath their feet but also in the hills and benches that rose on every side. In the space of a few hundred feet there was hidden gold worth several millions of dollars. The south fork of the creek was as yet unnamed, but there could be only one name for it: *Eldorado*.

But they did not linger here. Instead they hiked on up the narrowing valley, flushing a brown bear from the blueberry bushes, stumbling upon Joe Ladue's eleven-year-old camp-fires, panning periodically and finding a few colours in every pan, until they reached the dome that looked down over the land of the Klondike. Like Henderson, they were struck by the splendour of the scene that lay spread out before them like a Persian carpet: the little streams tumbling down the flanks of the great mountain, the hills crimson, purple, and emerald-green in the warm August sunlight (for already the early frosts were tinting trees and shrubs), the cranberry and salmonberry bushes forming a foreground fringe to the natural tapestry.

Below, in the narrow gorge of Gold Bottom Creek, a pale pillar of smoke marked Henderson's camp.

"Well, boys," said Carmack, "we've got this far, let's go down and see what they've got."

Skookum Jim hesitated; Henderson's remarks about Siwashes still bothered him. But in the end the trio clambered down the gorge to the camp where Henderson and his three companions were washing out gold from an open cut.

Exactly what happened between Carmack and Henderson has long been in dispute. Carmack later insisted that he urged Henderson to come over to Rabbit Creek and stake a claim. Henderson always swore that it was he who urged Carmack to prospect Rabbit – and if he found anything to let Henderson know.

Two facts are fairly clear. First, Carmack did promise Henderson that if he found anything worthwhile on Rabbit he would send word back; Henderson offered to pay him for his trouble if the occasion arose. Second, the Indians tried to purchase some tobacco from Henderson, and Henderson refused, possibly because he was short of supplies, but more likely because of his attitude towards Indians, since it was against his code to refuse a fellow prospector anything. This action was to cost him dearly.

Carmack tried the prospects at Gold Bottom, but did not stake, and the trio headed back over the mountain. The way was hard. They struggled over fallen trees and devil's clubs, a peculiarly offensive thorn, and they forced their way through tangled underbrush, brier roses, and raspberry bushes. On the far side of the mountain they floundered into a swamp that marked the headwaters of Rabbit Creek, and here they had to hop from clump to clump on their slippery moccasins or sink to their thighs in the glacial ooze. Hordes of gnats and mosquitoes rose about them as they stumbled on, unable to swat the insects for fear of losing their balance.

Thus they came wearily to the fork of Rabbit Creek once

more, and pressed on for about half a mile (0.8 km) before making camp for the night. It was August 16, the eve of a memorable day that is still celebrated as a festive holiday in the Yukon Territory.

Who found the nugget that started it all? Again, the record is blurred. Years afterward Carmack insisted it was he who happened upon the protruding rim of bedrock from which he pulled a thumb-sized chunk of gold. But Skookum Jim and Tagish Charley always claimed that Carmack was stretched out asleep under a birch tree when Jim, having shot a moose, was cleaning a dish-pan in the creek and made the find.

At any rate, the gold was there, lying thickly between the flaky slabs of rock like cheese in a sandwich. A single panful yielded a quarter of an ounce (12.5 g), or about four dollars' worth. In a country where a ten-cent pan had always meant good prospects, this was an incredible find. Carmack flung down the pan and let out a war-whoop, and the three men began to perform a wild dance around it – a sort of combination Scottish hornpipe, Indian foxtrot, Irish jig, and Siwash hula, as Carmack later described it. They collapsed, panting, smoked a cigarette apiece, and panned out some more gravel until Carmack had gathered enough coarse gold to fill an empty Winchester shotgun shell. Then they settled down for the night, the Indians chanting a weird song of praise into the embers of the fire while Carmack, staring at the dying flames, conjured up visions of wealth – of a trip around the world, of a suburban mansion rimmed with flower borders, of a suitcase full of gilt-edged stock certificates. In that instant of discovery something fundamental had happened to Siwash George: suddenly he had ceased to be an Indian. And he never thought of himself as an Indian again.

The following morning the trio staked claims on Rabbit Creek, which would soon be renamed Bonanza. Under Canadian mining law, no more than one claim may be staked in any mining district by anyone except the discoverer, who is allowed a double claim. Carmack blazed a small spruce tree with his hand-axe, and on the upstream side wrote with a pencil:

TO WHOM IT MAY CONCERN

I do, this day, locate and claim, by right of discovery,
five hundred feet, running up stream from this notice.
Located this 17th day of August, 1896.

G.W. Carmack

The claim, also by law, straddled the creek, and ran for five hundred feet (150 m). Carmack then measured off three more claims – one additional for himself, by right of discovery; *One Above* discovery for Jim; and another below for Charley, which, under the claim-numbering system, became *Two Below.* Jim's story, later, was that Carmack took the additional claim for himself, having persuaded Jim that, although he had made the discovery, as an Indian he would not be recognized as discoverer.

That done, and with no further thought of Robert Henderson, waiting for news on the far side of the hills, the three set off through the swamps to emerge five hours later on the Klondike again, their bodies prickling with thorns.

They had moved only a short distance downriver when they came upon four beaten and discouraged men wading knee-deep in the mud along the shoreline and towing a loaded boat behind them. These were Nova Scotians who had come to the Yukon Valley by way of California and had since tramped all over the territory without success. They were starving when they reached the Klondike looking for salmon, but here they had heard of Henderson's strike. Now, in the intense August heat, their hunger forgotten, they were dragging their supplies (or their "outfit," as it was known) upstream, searching once again for gold.

The leader, Dave McKay, asked Carmack if he had heard of Henderson's strike.

"I left there three days ago," Carmack said, holding his boat steady with a pike pole.

"What do you think of it?"

Carmack gave a slow, sly grin. "I don't like to be a knocker, but I don't think much of it."

The faces of the four men fell: all were now at the end of their tether.

Carmack meets a group of Nova Scotians tracking their boat up Bonanza Creek, heading for a new strike.

"You wouldn't advise us to go up there?" Dan McGillivery, one of the partners, asked.

"No," said Carmack, still grinning, "because I've got something better for you." With that, he pulled out his nugget-filled cartridge case, like a magician plucking a rabbit from a hat.

As the Nova Scotians' eyes goggled, Carmack gave them directions to his claim. Without further ado, the four men scrambled upriver, the tow-line on their boat as taut as a violin string. This chance meeting with Carmack made fortunes for all of them.

"I felt as if I had just dealt myself a royal flush in the game of life, and the whole world was a jackpot," Carmack later remarked, when recalling the incident.

He reached the salmon camp at the Klondike's mouth, and here he hailed two more discouraged men – Alphonse Lapierre of Quebec and his partner, another French Canadian. These two had been eleven years in the North, and now, en route downriver to Fortymile, almost starving, out of flour and bacon, their faces blistering in the sun, they had reached the low point of their careers.

"If I were you boys, I wouldn't go any further," Carmack told them as they beached their boat. "Haven't you heard of the new strike?"

"Oh yes, we know all about heem. I tink hees wan beeg bluff."

"How's this for bluff?" Carmack shouted, producing the gold. Again the effect was electric. The two men unloaded their boat, filled their packs, and fairly ran across the flat, waving their hands and chattering in a mixture of French and English. The abandoned boat would have floated off with the current if Carmack had not secured it.

As Carmack made preparations to set out for Fortymile to record his claim, he continued to tell anyone he encountered about the gold on Rabbit Creek. He made a special trip across the river to tell an old friend, then sent Jim back to guard the claims and drifted off with Tagish Charley down the Yukon, still spreading the news. He told everybody, including a man who on hearing the tale called him the biggest liar this side of hell.

One man Carmack did not tell. He sent not a whisper back to Robert Henderson.

CHAPTER THREE

The triumph of Lying George

L ATE IN THE AFTERNOON Carmack landed at the mining camp of Fortymile, near the Alaska border, and went straight to Bill McPhee's saloon. Fortymile was a weird and lonely village named for the river which flowed into the Yukon at that point, forty miles (64 km) north of Fort Reliance. It was totally remote from the world, existing for eight months out of twelve as if in a vacuum, its residents sealed off from the rest of civilization.

The nearest outfitting port was San Francisco, almost five thousand water miles (8,000 km) distant, and the only links with the sea were two cockleshell sternwheelers, the *New Racket*, and the Alaska Commercial Company's *Arctic*, built in 1889. These boats seldom had time to make more than one summer trip upstream from the old Russian seaport of St. Michael, near the river's mouth on the Bering Sea.

The little steamboats were the town's only lifeline. If one sank, the miners starved. On her maiden voyage in 1889, the *Arctic* was damaged and unable to bring supplies to

Fortymile. The A.C. Company sent Indian runners sixteen hundred miles (2,500 km) from the Bering Sea to the settlement to warn the miners that no supplies would be arriving, and that they must escape from the Yukon Valley or starve. As the October snows drifted down from the dark skies, the Fortymilers jammed aboard the *New Racket* , and the little vessel made a brave attempt to reach St. Michael at the Yukon's mouth before the river froze. She was caught in the ice floes 190 miles (305 km) short of her goal, and the hungry passengers had to continue the journey on foot. Those who remained at the community of Fortymile spent a hungry winter: indeed, one man lived for nine months on a steady diet of flapjacks.

There was one alternative route to the outside world, once winter set in. That was the gruelling trek upstream from Fortymile to the Chilkoot, more than six hundred miles (1,000 km) distant. It was seldom attempted. Four men who tried it in 1893 were forced to abandon fifteen thousand dollars in gold dust on the mountain slopes and were so badly ravaged by the elements that one died and another was crippled for life.

Who were these men who had chosen to wall themselves off from the world in a village of logs deep in the sub-Arctic wilderness? On the face of it, they were men chasing the will-o'-the-wisp of fortune – chasing it with an intensity and a determination that had brought them to the ends of the earth. But the evidence suggests the opposite. They seemed more like men pursued than men pursuing, and if they sought anything, it was the right to be left alone.

Bill McPhee's saloon was crowded with such men when Carmack arrived. Autumn was approaching and many had come in from their claims to acquire their winter outfits before snowfall. Behind the bar was Clarence Berry, a one-time fruit farmer from Fresno, California. He didn't know it, but Carmack's arrival and discovery would make him a wealthy man for the rest of his life.

Berry had gone north in 1894 as a last resort – a victim of the depression of the 1890s. He borrowed money at a high rate of interest to buy his outfit and passage. A giant of a man with the biceps of a blacksmith and the shoulders of a wrestler, his magnificent strength had sustained him when his fellows faltered. Out of a party of forty that had crossed the passes into the Yukon that year, only Berry and two others reached Fortymile. The rest had turned back discouraged after a storm destroyed their outfits.

But Berry wouldn't give up. He pushed ahead with little more than the clothes on his back. A year later he trekked back to California, married his childhood sweetheart, a sturdy waitress from Selma named Ethel Bush, and again headed for Alaska. He strapped his bride to a sleigh, which he dragged over the mountains and down the river. He found no gold, so he went to work tending bar for Bill McPhee, and it was here that he encountered Carmack.

Carmack was no drinking man, but on this occasion he felt the need for two whiskeys. It was not until he swallowed these that he was ready to break the news. After more than a decade his moment had come and he savoured it. He turned his back to the bar and raised his hand.

"Boys, I've got some good news to tell you. There's a big strike up the river."

"Strike, hell!" somebody shouted. "That ain't no news. That's just a scheme of Ladue and Harper to start a stampede up the river."

"That's where you're off, you big rabbit-eating malemute!" Carmack cried. "Ladue knows nothing about this." He pulled out his cartridge full of gold and poured it onto the "blower," upon which gold was weighed. "How does that look to you, eh?"

"Is that some Miller Creek gold that Ladue gave you?" someone asked sardonically.

A wave of suspicion swept the room. Nobody believed that Lying George had made a strike. Nevertheless, they crowded to the bar and examined the gold curiously. A seasoned prospector could tell from which creek a given amount of gold came simply by looking at it, and this gold was certainly strange. It did not come from Miller Creek, nor from Davis, nor from Glacier; it did not come from the bars of the Stewart or the Indian. In texture, shape, and colour, it was different from any gold that had been seen before in the Yukon Valley.

The men in Bill McPhee's saloon looked uneasily about them. All of them had been on stampedes before, and

In Bill McPhee's saloon at Fortymile, Carmack tells a sceptical crowd about his big strike.

almost all of those stampedes had led them up false trails. And yet . . .

One by one they started to slip away. Bewildered, some went to see William Ogilvie, the Canadian government surveyor, to ask his opinion, and Ogilvie pointed out that Carmack must have found the gold *somewhere*. That was enough.

Silently, in the twilight hours of the August night, one after another, the boats slid off. By morning Fortymile was a dead mining camp, empty of boats and empty of men. Even the drunks had been dragged from the saloons by their friends and tied down, protesting, in the boats that were heading for the Klondike.

Meanwhile, Carmack and Charley crossed the mouth of the Fortymile and went into the police post to record their claims. The recorder took one look at Lying George and laughed at him. Once again Carmack produced his shell full of gold dust. The recorder stopped laughing. From that moment on, few men laughed or called him Lying George again.

CHAPTER FOUR

Eldorado!

U P AND DOWN THE YUKON VALLEY the news spread like
a great stage-whisper. It moved as swiftly as the
breeze in the birches, and more mysteriously. Men squatting by nameless creeks heard the tale, dropped their pans,
and headed for the Klondike. Men seated by dying camp-
fires heard it and started up in the night, shrugging off
sleep to make tracks for the new strike. Men poling up the
Yukon towards the mountains or drifting down the Yukon
towards the wilderness heard it and did an abrupt about-
face in the direction of the salmon stream whose name no
one could pronounce properly.

Some did not hear the news at all but, drifting past the
Klondike's mouth, saw the boats and tents and the excited
figures, felt the hair rise on their necks, and then, still
unbelieving, joined the clamouring throng pushing up
through the weeds and muck of Rabbit Creek.

Joe Ladue already was on the scene. His quick merchant's
mind had swiftly grasped the situation. Others were scram-
bling to stake claims, but Ladue was more interested in

43

staking out a townsite on the swamp below the scarred mountain at the Klondike's mouth. That was the start of Dawson City. It was worth all the gold of Bonanza. Within two years, lots sold for as much as $5,000 a front foot on the main street.

Ladue headed for Fortymile to register his site, but on the way he met a man who wanted timber to build a house. Ladue's lively imagination saw a thousand houses rising on the swampland. Back in his tracks he turned, sending his application down to the police by runner. At his trading post at Sixtymile he loaded his raft with all the available dressed lumber, then floated his sawmill to the new town-site. Soon he had a rough warehouse built, and a little cabin for himself, which did duty as a saloon. It was the first building in the new mining camp, which Ladue had already named after George M. Dawson, a government geologist.

It was the old-timers who were skeptical of Bonanza. The valley was too wide, they said, and the willows did not lean the proper way, and the water did not taste right. It was too far upriver. It was on the wrong side of the Yukon. It was moose pasture. Only newcomers, known as "chee-chakos," were too green to realize that it could not contain gold. That made some of them rich.

The men who first staked the Klondike were men who saw it as a last chance – men in poor luck, sick and discouraged, with nothing better to do than follow the siren call of a new stampede. Many of these sold their claims in the first week, believing them worthless. Many more tried vainly to sell, so that in that first winter two-thirds of the richest properties in the Klondike could have been bought for a song. Most men were too poor to work their claims; they went back to Dawson or Fortymile to try to get jobs to raise funds. Others, infected by the excitement of the moment, simply wandered back and forth aimlessly up and down the valley.

Carmack himself could not start work at once. He was forced to cut logs for Ladue's mill to earn enough to feed himself. Even then he was so short of funds he could build only three lengths of sluicebox. As he had no wheelbarrow, he carried the gravel in a box on his back for one hundred feet (30 m) to the stream to wash out the gold. In spite of this awkward arrangement, he cleaned up fourteen hundred dollars from surface prospects in less than a month. It would be worth thirty times as much today. But even in the face of this evidence there were only a few men who believed that there actually was gold in the valleys of the Klondike.

By the end of August all of Bonanza Creek had been staked, and new prospectors, arriving daily, were fanning out across the Klondike watershed looking for more ground. None realized it, but the richest treasure of all still lay undiscovered.

Down Bonanza, in search of new ground, trudged a young Austrian immigrant named Antone Stander. For nine years, ever since he had landed in New York City, Stander had been seeking his fortune in the remote corners of the continent, working as a cowboy, as a sheep-herder, as a farmer, as a coal-miner, and now as a prospector. When he arrived in the New World, unable to speak a word of English, he had just $1.75 to his name. After mastering the language and walking over most of North America, he was no richer. All his funds had been spent on the trip north in the spring of 1896. Now, on this last day of August, he was embarking on a final gamble.

He was a handsome man, just 29 years old, with dark, curly hair and sensitive, romantic-looking features. As he reached the south fork of Bonanza Creek, a few hundred feet above Carmack's claim, he stopped to examine it curiously. Later Stander would look back upon this as the most important moment of his life, for after this day nothing was ever again the same for him. The narrow wooded ravine, with a trickle of water snaking along its bottom, still had no name. The prospectors referred to it in Yukon parlance as "Bonanza's pup." It would soon be known as Eldorado.

Stander arrived at the fork with four companions, all of whom had already staked on Bonanza. They had little faith in their property, but on an impulse they walked up the pup in a group and sank their pans into the sand. Like Stander, each had reached the end of the line financially. Now they stared into the first pan and, to their astonishment, saw that there was more than six dollars' worth of gold in the bottom. They had no way of knowing it, but this was the richest creek in the world. Each of the claims staked that day eventually produced one million dollars or more.

As Stander and his companions drove in their stakes, others up and down Bonanza began to sense by some curious kind of telepathy that something tantalizing was in the wind. Louis Emkins, a lean-faced and rangy prospector from Illinois, was struggling up Bonanza when he saw the campfires flickering among the bushes of the unexplored creek. It was enough to send the blood pulsing through his veins. He and his three companions quickened their pace and burst upon Stander and the others, who tried to discourage them, claiming that the prospects were small and only on the surface.

Two of the men turned back at once, a fortune slipping from their grasp, but Emkins and his partner George Demars stayed on. *Seven* had already been staked illegally for a friend in Fortymile, but Emkins, a determined figure with a forbidding black moustache, would have none of it. He tore up the stakes and substituted his own, and by that single action made himself wealthy. Within a year he was able to sell out for more than one hundred thousand dollars.

William Johns, a black-bearded and rawboned ex-newspaper reporter from Chicago, was at the mouth of the Eldorado when Emkins's two discouraged comrades emerged, talking disconsolately of "skim diggings" on a moose flat. Some sixth sense told Johns to prospect the pup anyway. He had a strange feeling that something important was afoot. This sensation increased when he met Emkins and Demars, who were suspiciously casual about their prospects, and then Frank Keller, Stander's companion, who was curiously evasive about what he had found.

When Johns and his three Norwegian companions headed up the new creek the following day, one of them pointed to the water:

"Someone's working; the water's muddy!"

The four men crept upstream, alert and silent – "like hunters who have scented game," as Johns put it. Suddenly

PAY DIRT

WASTE   SHAFT DIRT

FROZEN MOSS

PREHISTORIC CREEK BED
CONTAINING GOLD

FROZEN MUD

FROZEN GRAVEL

HARD PAN

GOLD BEARING SAND (PAY DIRT)

Cutaway Section of a Klondike Claim

they surprised Stander crouching over a panful of gold with three of his companions crowding about him. They looked "like a cat caught in a cream pitcher," and Johns and his friends needed no further encouragement to stake. One of the Norwegians who had read a great deal named the new creek Eldorado, more or less as a joke. But, as it turned out, the title fitted.

To the newcomers, however, this narrow cleft in the wooded hills was just another valley with good surface prospects. These really meant very little, for gold lying in

CACHE

DAM FOR
SUMMER
SLUICING

SLUICE BOX

THAWING
GROUND TO DIG

SLUICE

ACTUAL CREEK
BED DRY IN
THE WINTER

ROCKER BOX

PAN

the gravel on the creek's edge did not necessarily mean that the valley was rich. Before that could be determined, someone would have to go through the hard labour of building fires to burn one or more shafts down through the permafrost for at least fifteen feet (4.5 m) to bedrock, searching for the "pay-streak" (which might not exist). Then the muck must be hauled up by windlass to the surface and washed down a sluicebox to find out how much gold there really was.

The sluiceboxes were long, three-sided wooden troughs with crossbars, known as "riffles," and cocoa matting on the floor. By damming the creek and building up a head of water, the prospector could wash the paydirt down the incline of the sluicebox, shovelling it in from the "dump" that had been hoisted by buckets from the bottom of the shaft. The coarse gold was caught in the riffles, for it was nineteen times as heavy as the rushing water; the fine gold sank into the mesh of the cocoa matting. Every three days, the miners turned off the water from the dam, removed the gold and black sand from the riffles and matting.

The final "clean-up" as it was called, was done by panning the sand – an exhausting task that involved squatting on the ground and rotating the pan with a movement of the shoulders until the water had washed away the lighter sand, leaving the specks of glistening gold behind.

This back-breaking toil could easily occupy two months. Until the muck was washed down the sluicebox, it was pure guesswork to estimate a claim's true worth. Until the spring thaw came and the rushing creek provided enough head of water to wash the gravels drawn up the shaft that winter, no one could really say exactly how rich Eldorado was – if, indeed, it was rich at all.

Chapter Five

Robert Henderson's bad luck

MOST OF THE MEN who staked claims on the new creek in that first week had already done their share of prospecting. They had sunk shafts and shovelled gravel on creek after creek in the Yukon watershed without success. To them this little pup looked exactly like any other in the territory. If anything, it looked scrawnier and less attractive.

To most men, then, Eldorado was as much of a gamble as the Irish sweepstakes. Some, such as Stander, determined to take the gamble and hold their ground and work it to see whether it really did contain gold. Others decided to sell out at once for what they could get. Still others bravely set out to take the risk and then got cold feet and sold before the prize was theirs.

Nobody then knew, of course, that this was the richest placer creek in the world, that almost every claim from *One* to *Forty* was worth at least half a million, that some were worth three times that amount, and that half a century later dredges would still be taking gold from the worked-over gravels.

But in that first winter paper fortunes changed hands as easily as packages of cigarettes, and poor men became rich and then poor again without realizing it. Jay Whipple, for instance, sold claim *One* almost immediately, for a trifle. The purchaser, a lumberman from Eureka, California, named Skiff Mitchell, lived for half a century on the proceeds.

So the wheel of fortune spun around on Eldorado. Al Thayer and Winfield Oler had staked out *Twenty-nine* and, believing it worthless, returned to Fortymile, looking for a sucker on whom to unload it. They found one in Jimmy Kerry's saloon in the person of Charley Anderson, a 37-year-old Swede with a pinched face, who had been mining for several years out of Fortymile. Anderson was so doubtful of the Klondike that he had delayed his trip to the new field until all the ground was gone. Now he was drinking heavily, and Oler, a small and slender man from Baltimore, saw his chance. Anderson woke up the next morning to find he had bought an untried claim for $800.

Anderson went to the Mounted Police post to ask Inspector Charles Constantine to retrieve his money for him, but the policeman pointed out that his signature was on the title. Anderson glumly headed for Eldorado. He had no way of knowing yet that a million dollars' worth of gold lay in the bedrock under his claim and that for the rest of his life he would bear the tag of "the Lucky Swede." As for Oler, he became the butt of so many jokes that he fled the country in disgust.

And yet, who is to say which were the lucky ones in the Eldorado lottery? Many who sold out and left the country ended their lives in relative comfort. Many who stayed behind to dig out fortunes lost all in the end. William Sloan, a Nanaimo dry-goods merchant, sold his interest in *Fifteen* for $50,000 and turned his back on the Klondike forever. He invested his money wisely and rose to become a cabinet minister in British Columbia's provincial government. His son became Chief Justice of that province. But the Lucky Swede died penniless and alone.

All this while, on the other side of the Bonanza watershed, Robert Henderson continued to toil at his open cut on the creek he had wistfully name Gold Bottom. Boats were arriving daily at Dawson; shacks were being clapped together helter-skelter on valley and mud flat; Bonanza was staked for fourteen miles (22.5 km) and Eldorado for three (5 km); and men were spraying across the whole of the Klondike country searching for new discoveries.

Henderson knew nothing of this; he had seen no one but his partners since that August day when Carmack had gone off, promising to send word back if he found anything on the other side of the blue hills.

Then one day – some three weeks after the strike – Henderson looked up and saw a group of men coming down from the divide. He asked them where they had come from, and they replied: "Bonanza Creek."

The name puzzled Henderson, who prided himself on a knowledge of the country. He did not like to show his ignorance, but finally curiosity overcame pride. Where was Bonanza Creek?

The newcomers pointed back over the hill.

"Rabbit Creek! What have you got there?" Henderson asked, with a sinking feeling.

"We have the biggest thing in the world."

"Who found it?"

"McCormick."

Henderson flung down his shovel, then walked slowly over to the bank of the creek and sat down. It was some time before he could speak. McCormick! *Carmack!* For the rest of his life the sound of that name would be like a cold knife in his heart. Why, the man was not even a prospector!

When he gathered his wits about him, Henderson realized that he must record a claim at once before the human overflow from Bonanza arrived at his creek. He had explored a large fork of Gold Bottom and discovered much better ground yielding thirty-five cents to the pan. Here he had staked a discovery claim, and it was this that he intended to record at Fortymile. He divided up his small gleanings of gold with his partners and set off at once.

But fate had not yet finished with Robert Henderson. He had moved only a short way down the creek before he encountered two long-time prospectors. He knew them both. One was Charles Johnson, tall, bearded, and tough, a farmer and logger from Ohio; the other was Andrew Hunker, better known as "Old Man Hunker," a native of

Wittenberg, Germany, a man with sharp features and a dogged face who made a practice of reading Gibbon's *Decline and Fall of the Roman Empire* nightly. (Indeed, he carried six volumes about with him.) Both men were veteran prospectors of the Yukon Valley.

Hunker now revealed to Henderson that he, too, had staked a discovery claim on the other fork of Gold Bottom Creek. The partners had got as much as $2.50 a pan from a reef of high bedrock, and they were carrying twenty-five dollars' worth of coarse gold with them, all of it panned out in a few minutes. Obviously the Hunker claims were far richer than the ones Henderson had staked.

What was Henderson to do? A discovery claim was twice the size of an ordinary claim. He could insist on his own earlier discovery and take a thousand feet (305 m) of relatively poor ground. But the richer ground was obviously in the area of Hunker's find. The only answer was to allow Hunker the discovery claim and for Henderson to stake an ordinary claim of five hundred feet next to it. Thus the entire watershed became known as Hunker Creek, and only the fork which Henderson originally located was called Gold Bottom.

Henderson, having swallowed this second bitter pill, pushed on down the Klondike Valley. Soon a new prize was dangled before him. He ran into a Finn named Solomon Marpak who had just made a discovery on another tributary of the Klondike called Bear Creek. Henderson staked next to Marpak, his spirits rising; Bear Creek looked rich.

He now believed he had three claims to record – on Gold Bottom, on Hunker, and on Bear – but when he reached Fortymile, fate dealt him a third blow. He was told that the law had been changed. No man was allowed more than one claim in the Klondike mining district, and that claim must be recorded within sixty days of staking. In vain Henderson protested that when he had staked his ground the law had allowed a claim on each creek, with no deadline for recording. The mining recorder did not know him. Henderson swallowed hard and recorded only the Hunker Creek claim.

"I only want my just dues and nothing more, but those discoveries rightly belong to me and I will contest them as a Canadian as long as I live," he said with force and bitterness. And so began the long controversy over which man was the rightful discoverer of the Klondike. It rages still, and almost always along national lines: the English and Canadians say that Henderson should have the credit; the Americans stand by Carmack.

C LARENCE BERRY QUIT HIS JOB as bartender in Fortymile and was one of those who left town immediately on hearing Carmack's news. He was helped by his old boss, Bill McPhee, the owner of the saloon, who lent him enough money to buy food to keep him going. When Berry reached Bonanza Creek he was able to stake claim number *Forty Above* discovery. It wasn't a terribly rich claim, but it wasn't a poor one either. Berry's real fortune lay ahead, however. He owed it to Antone Stander, the Austrian who had staked on Eldorado.

The handsome Stander was back in Fortymile, without funds, without food, and, to his pain and bewilderment, without credit at the Alaska Commercial Company's store, which wouldn't advance him any provisions until he got somebody to back him. Stander was desperately seeking a friend when Berry volunteered to help. In gratitude, Stander gave him half of his Eldorado property in exchange for half of the claim that Berry had staked on Bonanza. With that simple gesture Clarence Berry laid the foundation for one of the largest personal fortunes to come out of the Klondike.

That fall, while Ladue's sawmill was turning out rough lumber for the first of Dawson's buildings, while Carmack was treating his friends to drinks in the tent saloons at fifty dollars a round, while old-timers continued to jeer and newcomers scouted the valleys for new ground, the industrious Berry and one or two others set about the slow work of burning shafts to bedrock to find out just how much gold there was in the Klondike Valley.

On *Twenty-one Above* Bonanza, Louis Rhodes was also reluctantly grubbing his way down through the frozen muck. He felt a bit of a fool, for his neighbours were laughing at him, but when he tried to sell out for $250 there were no takers, and so he kept working. On October 3, at a depth of fifteen feet (4.6 m), he reached bedrock.

The results were electrifying. In the soft rock he could spy, by guttering candlelight, broad seams of clay and gravel streaked with gold. This was the "pay-streak." He had hit the old creek channel squarely on his first try. It was so rich that he was able to hire workmen on the spot and to pay them nightly by scooping up a few panfuls of dirt from the bottom of the shaft.

Heartened by this news, Berry kept working until, early in November, he too reached bedrock. From a single pan of paydirt he weighed out $57 in gold and knew at once that his days of poverty were over. (Gold in those days was worth $16 an ounce. Today the price is close to four hun-

Louis Rhodes sinks his shaft to bedrock and strikes it rich.

dred dollars.) He and Stander began to hire men to help them haul the dirt up by windlass and pile it on the great "dump" which, when the spring thaw came, would be shovelled into sluiceboxes so that the gold could be washed free of the clay and gravel.

Berry and Stander were also able to pay their workmen with gold dug out on the spot. They bought the two adjoining claims, *Four* and *Five*, from the original stakers of Eldorado and eventually split this block of claims in half, Stander taking the lower half and Berry the upper. Berry alone took $140,000 from his winter dump the following spring.

Now the Klondike was a frenzy of excitement as every claim-owner began to burrow into the frozen earth. Glowing in the long nights with a hundred miners' fires, the valleys looked like the inferno itself. Those who had scoffed at Rhodes and Berry could now peer down their shafts and literally see the nuggets glittering in the candle's rays.

Meanwhile a tent town was forming along the margin of the Yukon near the mouth of the Klondike River. By January there were only four houses in Dawson besides Ladue's, but the tents, like dirty white sails, were scattered in ragged order between the trees on the frozen swampland. It was not an ideal townsite, but it was close to the source of gold.

No one in the outside world yet knew of the existence of the new camp or of the gold that nourished it. In Fortymile, William Ogilvie, the Canadian government surveyor, was searching about for some means to inform his government of the situation.

Scarcely anyone would attempt the dangerous journey up the river to the Chilkoot Pass, but Captain William Moore, a remarkably tough 73-year-old, offered to take a short message. Moore was a steamboat man who had been in almost every gold rush from Peru to the Cassiars and who now made his home on Skagway Bay, at the foot of the Coast Mountains. At an age when most men were over the hill of life, the white-bearded old pioneer was still going strong. He had a contract to bring the Canadian mail across the mountains and into the interior of the Yukon, and when his U.S. counterpart failed to deliver, Moore took on his job too.

That fall of 1896, Moore had already been down the river to Circle City (in Alaska) and was now heading back again like a man on a Sunday jaunt when he picked up Ogilvie's message. Moore put all other mushers to shame; three young men, strong and vigorous, had all started from Fortymile the previous week in an attempt to make a record trip to the coastal Panhandle. When the aged mail-carrier overtook the trio, they were exhausted and starving. Moore popped them onto his dog-sled and whisked them out to Juneau without further mishap. As far as Ogilvie was concerned, the trip, though memorable, was a waste of time. His report went on to Ottawa, where nobody paid any attention to it.

As the town of Dawson slowly took shape around Ladue's

sawmill and saloon, a subtle change began to work among those prospectors who for years had had nothing to call their own. Accepted standards of wealth vanished. There was a desperate shortage of almost everything that a man needed, from nails to women. But there was no shortage of gold. Those who had struck it rich could claw the legal tender from the dumps with their bare hands; and thus, to many, gold became the cheapest commodity in the world.

No other community on the earth had a greater percentage of would-be millionaires. Yet all its citizens were living under worse conditions than any sharecropper. Food became so scarce that all but the most expensive dogs had to be killed because the owners did not have enough to feed them. Only the fortunate arrival of a raftload of beef cattle saved the camp from starvation. Willis Thorpe, a Juneau butcher, sold the meat for $16,000; within a year he was worth $200,000.

There was no writing paper in Dawson and nothing to read. The only eggs came from two hens owned by a policeman's wife, and these cost a dollar apiece. Laundry was so expensive that most men wore their shirts until they couldn't stand them any longer and then threw them away. One French Canadian turned a net profit by retrieving these garments, laundering them, and reselling them, often enough to the former owners. The camp's single bathhouse consisted of a small tent with a stove and an up-ended log as a stool; for five minutes in a wooden laundry tub the unclean paid a dollar and a half.

The ante at stud poker was one dollar, but it might easily cost five hundred to see the third card. A night on the town – which meant a night in Joe Ladue's bare-boarded saloon, drinking watered whiskey – could cost at least fifty dollars. Few minded the expense; it was so easy to pan out a few shovelfuls of dirt from the dump to pay for the fun.

One man went to work in the morning and came to town at night with fourteen hundred dollars in gold. In Ladue's he ordered two whiskeys, toasting his former self in the one and making believe his former self was drinking the other, then stuck two cigars in his mouth and smoked them together.

This behaviour was less peculiar than it seemed. Every man's life had been changed by the strike. On the day he reached the pay-streak and realized that he was rich, he became a different person. Some men could no longer eat or sleep at the thought of mining so much gold. One, who had washed out thirty thousand dollars, became so obsessed by the fear of being robbed that he suffered a mental collapse and shot himself.

By midwinter the frenzied staking on the creeks had brought about a state of complete confusion. The original staking of Bonanza had been so unorganized that both the ownership and size of many claims were in dispute. Work stopped; men argued and fought; by January, when William Ogilvie arrived to survey the Ladue townsite, the miners begged him to re-survey Bonanza and Eldorado. Ogilvie agreed on the condition that his decisions should be accepted as final.

Few men were better fitted for the task of unsnarling the Klondike tangle, where the shifting of stakes by a few feet might mean the loss or gain of thousands of dollars. No one would dare to bribe Ogilvie. He firmly believed that no government servant should enrich himself because of his job. Alone among hundreds, he stubbornly refused to stake an inch of ground or to turn a single cent of profit from the Klondike strike. The sense of what was right had become an act of faith with Ogilvie, and he insisted that his son, Morley, who was with him, keep the same standard. Only one other man in the Yukon felt the same way, and that was Charles Constantine, the North West Mounted Police superintendent, who also left the country poor but respected, though some of his constables staked out fortunes.

With his round, solemn face and his dark beard, Ogilvie had the features that were later to be associated with reigning British monarchs, but this solemn appearance masked a puckish sense of humour. His whole character, indeed, was an unlikely mixture. The face that he presented to the public was that of the dedicated government official, conscientious and sedate. But in private he was a clever mimic, a punster, a practical joker, and a good storyteller known also for his ability to play anything on the piano, especially Scottish reels.

He went about his tasks on Bonanza and Eldorado with

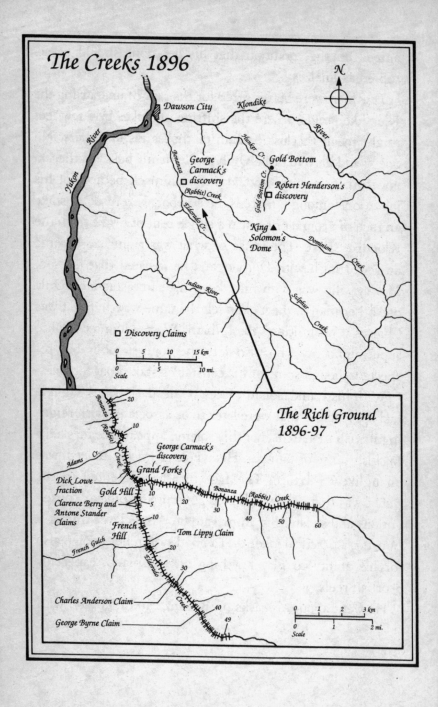

The Creeks 1896

N

Dawson City
Klondike
River

Yukon River

Hunker Cr.
George Carmack's discovery
Gold Bottom

Gold Bottom Cr.
Robert Henderson's discovery

(Rabbit) Creek

Eldorado Cr.

King Solomon's Dome

Dominion Creek

Indian River

Sulphur Creek

□ Discovery Claims

0   5   10   15 km

0   5   10 mi.

Scale

The Rich Ground 1896-97

Bonanza (Rabbit) Creek
20
10

Adams Cr.

George Carmack's discovery

Grand Forks

Dick Lowe fraction

Gold Hill

Clarence Berry and Antone Stander Claims

French Hill

Bonanza   (Rabbit)   Creek

10
5
20
30
40
50
60

10

French Gulch

Tom Lippy Claim

20

Eldorado Creek

30

Charles Anderson Claim

George Byrne Claim

40

49

0   1   2   3 km

0   1   2 mi.

Scale

professional seriousness, for his tidy civil servant's mind was shocked by the raggedness of the original staking. At the same time he carefully filed away in the neat pigeon-holes of his memory a small collection of anecdotes which served him as after-dinner stories in the years that followed. He was both dismayed and amused, for instance, to discover the way in which one prospector – a Mounted Policeman at that – had located a claim in the twisting section of Lower Bonanza. Instead of measuring off five hundred feet in a straight line, he followed the creek, which doubled back on itself in such a way that, when Ogilvie surveyed it, he discovered that the unfortunate policeman had got eight feet (2.4 m) *less* than a claim.

CHAPTER SEVEN

A friend in need

O GILVIE HAD MANY STORIES to tell about that first wild year. As the maximum legal stake was five hundred feet, many oversize claims were chopped down by his survey, leaving thin wedges of land sandwiched in between the new boundaries. These fractional claims could be very valuable: one on Eldorado, for instance, just ten feet (3 m) wide, was thought to be worth between ten and twenty thousand dollars.

And another, a mere five inches (12.7 cm) wide, was sold to the owner of the adjacent claim for five hundred dollars. Jim White, an Irishman from Circle City, Alaska, was convinced there was a fraction between *Thirty-Six* and *Thirty-Seven* Eldorado. He staked it and used the ground in an effort to bully the owners on either side to come to terms with him. He waited on tenterhooks for Ogilvie's survey to set the proper dimensions. In order to madden White, whom he considered a scoundrel and a blackmailer, Ogilvie deliberately delayed the work. When the ground was finally surveyed, the fraction turned out to be just three inches

(7.6 cm) wide. For the rest of his days its owner smarted under the nickname of Three-Inch White.

It was a bitterly cold spring day, about ten below zero (-23° C), and a biting wind was whistling up the trough of Eldorado when Ogilvie reached the upper limit of Clarence Berry's *Five*. Dusk was falling, and, as his assistants gathered up his instruments, the surveyor stood working out the figures in his notebook to see how long the claim really was. Around was gathered the usual group of miners, all guessing at the claim's size; for months they had been searching and measuring on their own, hoping without success to discover a fraction on Eldorado.

Now Ogilvie whistled in surprise when he discovered that *Five* was forty-one feet, six inches (12.6 m) too long. It was on this section of his claim, and this section only – one of the richest locations in the history of placer mining – that Berry had done his winter's work. Hundred-dollar pans were the rule here; five-hundred-dollar pans were not unusual. Now it turned out that Berry didn't own this rich sliver of land. And he could not stake it because he had used up his staking rights. His entire dump of paydirt stood on the fraction; it could not be washed out until spring. Meanwhile, anyone could stake it.

Ogilvie realized at once that, if he announced the fraction, Berry would lose everything he had worked for that winter, and also that a riot would probably follow as dozens fought to stake ground known to be worth hundreds of thousands. And now in that conscientious mind, so used to

William Ogilvie re-surveys the claims on Bonanza Creek.

the rule book, a struggle ensued; should he cling to procedure and take the consequences, or should he depart from the rigid path he had set himself? His solemn, bearded face did not change expression as, turning to Berry, who was standing nearby, he said: "Let's go to supper. I'm cold enough and hungry enough to eat nuggets."

A ripple of suspicion ran through the throng, and Berry sensed it as Ogilvie hurried towards the cabin.

"Is there anything wrong, Mr. Ogilvie?"

"Come out of hearing," the surveyor whispered. He had made his decision.

"What's wrong?" cried Berry, in an agony of impatience. "My God, what's wrong?"

Ogilvie maintained his cracking pace. "There's a fraction of forty-one feet, six inches on claim number five, and nearly all your winter's work is on it."

"My God!" Berry almost shouted. "What will I do?"

Ogilvie's civil servant mask returned. "It is not my place to advise you," he said. And then – another rent in the rule book: "Haven't you a friend you can trust?"

"Trust – how?"

"Why, to stake that fraction tonight and transfer it to yourself and partner."

Berry thought at once of George Byrne, who was at work on a claim five miles (8 km) up Eldorado. He rushed to the cabin, told his wife to get supper for Ogilvie, then dashed up the creek.

He returned with Byrne about half past nine and, in the

presence of a baffled Mrs. Berry, a strange little act took place. The two men carefully questioned Ogilvie about the proper method of legally staking a fraction, and Ogilvie replied politely. There was no suggestion that this was anything but an academic discussion, but the surveyor took the trouble to draw a detailed plan of the method of staking on a sheet of wrapping-paper, which he handed to Byrne.

In the small hours of the morning Byrne staked the fraction, which in that single season produced for Berry $140,000; in return Byrne got an equal length off the lower unworked end of the property so that Berry's block of land would remain unbroken. As Ogilvie wrote, "A friend like that, in such a need, is a friend indeed."

Ogilvie himself later that spring washed out a pan of dirt taken at random from Berry's shaft. On it was 119 dollars' worth of gold, or, as he remarked, "about half a year's salary for many a good clerk."

And yet Berry and his wife lived under the most primitive of conditions in a twelve-by-sixteen foot (3.7 m by 4.9 m) hovel without floor or windows, whose only furniture was two home-made chairs and two rickety bedsteads built of unplaned lumber and curtained with calico. By the door stood a sheet-iron stove which the Berrys had packed in over the trail. Beside it was the panning-tank of dirty water in which one of Berry's twenty-five workmen periodically tested the paydirt. A small glass kerosene lamp and a pair of copper gold-scales supplied the only other ornament.

The gold was everywhere. The wages Berry paid totalled

$150 a day, which he washed out himself each evening. When Mrs. Berry needed pocket-money, she merely walked to the dump and with a sharp stick, smashed apart the frozen clods and pulled out the nuggets. One day she went to call her husband for supper and, while she was waiting for him to come up the shaft, picked up fifty dollars' worth of coarse gold.

Ethel Berry's only female neighbour was Tom Lippy's wife, Salome, a sinewy little woman from Kinsman, Ohio, who lived with her husband in another tiny mud-roofed cabin, about a mile (1.6 km) up the valley. Lippy, like Berry, was industrious, sober, level-headed – and lucky. A sudden and inspired hunch had brought him to the Yukon.

He had started life as an iron-moulder in Pennsylvania, but his almost fanatical belief in physical culture had led him into the YMCA and then west to Seattle as a physical-training instructor. As a volunteer fireman he had once held the title of world's champion hose-coupler. Like everybody else who came in over the trail, he was tough: solidly built, dark, good-looking, and clean-shaven. An injury to his knee had forced his retirement from the YMCA, and a strange intuition had sent him north in 1896 on borrowed money. Now he had one of the richest claims in the Klondike. Although this was the most memorable winter of Thomas Lippy's life, it certainly was not the happiest, for the Klondike, which gave him his fortune, took the life of his adopted son who was drowned in the Yukon River. Not all the gold in Eldorado could have saved him.

CHAPTER EIGHT
The end of the line

T HE WINTER PASSED SLOWLY, dream-like for many. It was hard sometimes to separate reality from fantasy. In their dark hovels, the miners watched in fascination and disbelief as the small heaps of gold piled up in jars and bottles on the windowsills. It supplied the only ornament on the naked walls, glittering in the flat light of the sunless noons, or in the flickering of hoarded candles.

But with the coming of the summer of 1897, Dawson was to become front page news, its isolation from the world at an end. The camp waited impatiently for the arrival of the first steamboat in June. The Klondike's newly rich were ready to return to a civilization that some had rejected ten years before. There were more than eighty, each owning a fortune that ran from twenty-five thousand to half a million dollars.

Some were determined to leave the North forever and had already sold the claims, content to live modestly but securely for the rest of their lives. Others were looking for a brief celebration in the big cities of the Pacific coast before returning to the Klondike for more treasure. All felt the desperate need to escape from the dark confines of their cabins and tents and from the smoky depths of their mine shafts, just as they had once felt a similar need to escape the smoky, populous cities.

Then, early in June, a shrill whistle was heard out in the river, and the Alaska Commercial Company's tiny stern-wheeler *Alice* rounded the Moosehide Bluff and puffed into shore. The entire town poured down to greet her. She was loaded with equal quantities of liquor and food, and the whole community went on a spree, as every saloon served free drinks across the counter. A couple of days later a second steamboat, *Portus B. Weare*, arrived, and the performance was repeated. When the two boats left for the trip downstream, they carried with them the men who would bring the first news of the great strike out to the unsuspecting world. When the Klondikers finally reached Seattle and San Francisco they were mobbed by would-be gold-seekers.

One prospector, J.C. Miller of Los Angeles, was reduced to a state of nervous prostration by the swarms of gold-crazy men who visited him. Another, William Hewitt, who came out with a five-gallon (22 L) can filled with dust and nuggets, received more than a hundred callers a day for weeks, and letters from every state in the union.

But Ladue had perhaps the most frantic time of all, for

the papers quickly dubbed him Mayor of Dawson City, and he was pursued by such a throng of reporters, well-wishers, fortune-hunters, and cranks, that he fled to the East. He stepped off the train in Chicago into the arms of another waiting mob, and even when he reached his farm at Plattsburg in the Adirondacks of New York state there was no relief. A bushel basket full of mail awaited him. The people crowded into the parlour and began to finger the nuggets that he poured onto a table. Ladue left them to it and went off into a barn to hide. Here he was cornered by Lincoln

Steffens, the most persistent reporter of his day. "He was the weariest looking man I ever saw," Steffens wrote in *McClure's*.

It was a prophetic remark, for Ladue's days were numbered. His life reached its climax in a Cinderella ending, made to order for the press. At long last he married Anna Mason, his lifelong sweetheart, whose parents were now more than happy to welcome the most renowned figure in America into the family.

Ladue's name by this time was a household word. He was

The sternwheeler Alice, *first boat into Dawson in 1897, is greeted by a raucous crowd, many of them millionaires.*

Joe Ladue, the "Mayor of Dawson," thrills his friends and family by displaying his treasure at his home in Plattsburg, N.Y.

worth, on paper, five million dollars. His picture appeared in advertisements endorsing Dr. Green's Nervura blood and nerve remedy. The financial pages were soon reporting that he had been named president and managing director of the Joseph Ladue Gold Mining and Development Company, whose directors included some of the biggest names in New York finance.

Alas, for Ladue, the thirteen winters spent along the Yukon had taken their toll. A few months after he came out of the North, his aging partner, Arthur Harper, who had followed him down the coast in the next boat, died of tuberculosis. The following year Ladue also succumbed to the disease, at the height of the great stampede he helped bring about.

And what of Robert Henderson, the man whose tip to Carmack had started it all? Tragically his troubles never ended. The old injury to his leg prevented him from doing any work on his claim on Hunker Creek. All through the fall and winter he lay ill from that injury. And then he was off again, searching for gold. A less restless man might have gone to work on the Hunker claim, which was obviously a good one, but it was typical of Henderson that he ignored it in order to search for new gold-fields.

He trudged the length of Too Much Gold Creek, which contained no gold at all, and then, still supremely optimistic, headed for the Stewart River country. Here, too, he searched in vain, though he left his name behind on one of the Stewart's smaller tributaries.

At last he decided to return to his wife and children in Colorado, whom he had not seen for four years. He boarded a steamboat for St. Michael, anxious to be away, and here, for the fifth time, bad luck descended upon him. The steamer was frozen in at Circle City, and Henderson, trapped in the country which had brought him nothing but misfortune, fell sick again. In order to pay his medical bills he was forced to sell his claim on Hunker Creek. He received $3,000 for it; that represented the total amount that he took from the Klondike district. Yet each of the claims that he had staked and tried to record was worth a great deal. The Hunker claim eventually paid a royalty of $450,000, after which it was sold for another $200,000. For decades it continued to be a valuable property, but Henderson got none of it.

He reached St. Michael ultimately, the following spring, and boarded a steamer for Seattle. He had eleven hundred dollars left in Klondike gold, but his troubles were still not over. The years spent in the country of the open cabin door had not equipped him for civilization's wiles. Before he reached Seattle all his gold had been stolen. Disgusted, he tore an emblem from his lapel and handed it to Tappan Adney, the correspondent for *Harper's Illustrated Weekly*.

"Here, you keep this," he cried. "I will lose it, too. I am not fit to live among civilized men."

Adney examined the little badge curiously. It was the familiar insignia of an exclusive lodge, the Yukon Order of

Pioneers, with its golden rule and its motto: "Do unto others as you would be done by."

The statistics regarding the Klondike stampede are diminishing ones. One hundred thousand persons, it is estimated, actually set out on the trail; some thirty or forty thousand reached Dawson. Only about one half of this number bothered to look for gold, and of these only four thousand found any. Of the four thousand, a few hundred found gold in quantities large enough to call themselves rich. And out of these fortunate men only the merest handful managed to keep their wealth.

The kings of Eldorado toppled from their thrones one by one. Antone Stander drank part of his fortune away; his wife – a one-time dance-hall girl – deserted him and took the rest, including the Stander Hotel, which he had built in Seattle with profits from his claim. One cannot entirely blame her, for when Stander was drinking he was subject to crazy fits of jealousy; on one occasion he tried to cut her to pieces with a knife. Stander headed north again, seeking another Klondike, working his passage aboard ship by peeling potatoes in the galley, but he got no farther than the Alaskan Panhandle. He died in the Pioneers' Home at Sitka. His wife, who lived until 1944, left an estate worth fifty thousand dollars.

Win Oler died in the Pioneers' Home, too, plagued to the last by the knowledge that he had sold a million-dollar claim to the Lucky Swede for eight hundred dollars. But

Charley Anderson, the Lucky Swede, fared no better. His dance-hall girl wife divorced him; the 1906 San Francisco earthquake shattered his fortune, since he had invested heavily in real estate.

He remained, in spite of these setbacks, an incurable optimist, so convinced he would strike it rich again that he vowed never to shave off his little pointed beard until he became wealthy again. He was still wearing it in 1939 when he died, pushing a wheelbarrow in a sawmill near Sapperton, British Columbia, for $3.25 a day. It had always annoyed him when people referred to him as a millionaire. "I never had a million dollars," the Lucky Swede used to say. "The most I ever had was nine hundred thousand."

It is pleasant, in the light of all this, to report that the two most industrious men on Bonanza and Eldorado enjoyed continued success and fortune for the rest of their lives. Louis Rhodes and Clarence Berry, who sank the first two shafts to bedrock in the Klondike while their fellows twiddled their thumbs, did not squander their riches but, on the contrary, added to them.

Berry took $1,500,000 from his claims on Eldorado. Then he and his brothers moved on to Fairbanks, where they struck it rich a second time on Esther Creek. They returned to California, purchased oil property near Bakersfield, and made another enormous fortune. At various times they owned both the Los Angeles and the San Francisco baseball clubs.

Berry never forgot his original benefactor, Bill McPhee,

the saloon-keeper. In 1906 McPhee's saloon at Fairbanks was destroyed by fire, and the aging barkeeper lost everything but the clothes he wore. Berry wired him from San Francisco to draw on him for all the money necessary to get back into business again. In his declining years McPhee lived on pension from Berry, who died of appendicitis in San Francisco in 1930, worth several millions.

Louis Rhodes invested his Klondike fortune in mining property in Mexico and lost everything. Without a moment's hesitation he turned prospector again and headed for Alaska. With all the industry that he had shown in the early Bonanza days he began to explore the newly staked country near Fairbanks. He found gold-bearing quartz on a tiny outcropping of unstaked land and parlayed it into a mine that yielded him a profit of three hundred thousand dollars. He retired to California's Valley of the Moon and lived out the rest of his days in comfort.

And what of the original discoverers of the Klondike? Carmack abandoned his Indian wife, Kate, in 1900. She had not been able to cope with civilization and returned to her home at Caribou Crossing on Lake Tagish where she lived on a government pension, still wearing her cheap cotton clothing, but always with a necklace of nuggets taken from the famous claim on Bonanza. She died about 1917.

Carmack was married again to a pretty dark woman named Marguerite Laimee, who had been on the fringe of three gold rushes – in South Africa, Australia, and the Klondike. She and Carmack lived happily until his death in

Vancouver in 1922. He died wealthy and respected, and his wife inherited his money.

Tagish Charley sold his mining properties in 1901 and spent the rest of years at Carcross on the Yukon-B.C. border, where he operated a hotel, entertained lavishly and bought diamond earrings for his daughter. He was treated as a white man and allowed to drink heavily. As a result, one day when he was on a drunken spree, he fell off a bridge and was drowned.

Skookum Jim was treated as a white man too – but that was not enough for him. He wanted to *be* a white man. And so, although his mining property was paying him royalties of ninety thousand dollars a year, he continued to live the hard life of the prospector, travelling ceaselessly across the North vainly seeking a quartz load, often going for days without food, so fierce was his quest. In the end his magnificent physique was weakened. He died, worn out, in 1916.

Robert Henderson outlived them all. The Canadian government at last recognized him as a co-discoverer of the Klondike. It awarded him a pension of $200 a month. But for the rest of his life he continued to look for gold. He sought it on Vancouver Island, in Northern British Columbia, and on the Pelly River. In 1932 he joined two mining promoters in a gold discovery on the Upper Pelly. A party was organized to fly into the area on a prospecting trip. When the time came, he was not with them. He died of cancer in January of 1933, still talking of the big strike he hoped to make.

Index

Also Available
THE KLONDIKE STAMPEDE

The world's last great gold rush began in 1897 when one hundred thousand men and women dropped everything in the hopes of finding treasure in a far-off Yukon valley. The focus of their quest was so remote and so isolated that each gold-seeker was forced to carry almost one tonne of goods across the Chilkoot and White Passes.

In this second instalment of *The Great Klondike Gold Rush* series, Pierre Berton also tells of the fleet of more than seven thousand home-made boats, built in the mountain lakes and floated eight hundred kilometres downriver to Dawson, "The City of Gold."